PRAISE FOR YOU CAN'T FRY CHICKEN IN 8 MINUTES. . .

This book was inspiring and kept my attention. I read it in one sitting, and I'm a college student. It's great to read for some inspiration and motivation!

Lisa Copland
Student
Quinnipiac University

Wow! Thank you, Patrick, for making a hard to grasp concept real through your personal stories and examples. As a school counselor, I am THRILLED to have a fantastic resource to help guide my students to setting and reaching "Incredible Goals!" I highly recommend this book to all educators and students. Again. . . Wow!

Townsend Duane
School Counselor

With these simple steps, many incredible goals are within my reach.

Eric Sanford
Youth Pastor

Patrick uses real stories that inspire and motivate readers of all ages to improve their lives by giving them the confidence to set goals and the steps to accomplish them.

Katherine Johnson
Intervention Coordinator
Henrico County Schools

YOU CAN'T FRY CHICKEN IN 8 MINUTES

but you can set **Incredible Goals** in 8 steps

PATRICK GEORGE

You Can't Fry Chicken in 8 Minutes
but You Can Set Incredible Goals in 8 Steps

Written by Patrick M. George

Cover art by Lynda Ray

Edited by Jennifer Arndt

Layout/Design by Christi George

Photos by Backwater Photography

ISBN 978-1-4507-5565-8

Printed in the United States by instantpublisher.com

DEDICATION

I would like to dedicate this book to two of my mentors that have influenced my speaking and writing career that are no longer with us. . . Mr. Arnie Warren and Dr. Earl Reum.

I would also like to dedicate this book to all of the people that have my first two books.

ACKNOWLEDGMENTS

First, I would like to thank my wife, Christi, who has been so supportive during this entire book writing process. Thank you babe!

Secondly, I would have to thank Jennifer Arndt, my editor. Jennifer read this book as many (or more) times than I have. Jennifer . . . your patience and diligence during this project was priceless. I am 100% sure this book would not be a reality without your input and energy. I cannot thank you enough for what you brought to the table in the writing of this book. Simply put, you are "incredible".

Next, I would have to publicly thank Amy Schmucker. Your consistent motivation during this project is well appreciated. I will be calling you again when I start writing the next book. Thank you for all of the phone calls and emails.

I would like to thank the following people for their input in the exhausting review process: Jeffery Katz, Abi Arndt, Leen Doumet, Lisa Copland, Harriett Turk, Kalisha George and Melissa Sohn.

A special thanks goes to my "Jewish" mother, Marion Sherman for her page-by-page review with love.

Thank you to Chris Thompson "Iceman" for his candid input.

Thank you to Townsend Duane for her honest "late-night" thoughtful insight and input.

Great big thanks to Lynda Ray who created the awesome cover artwork. She taught me something with a mere drawing.

If I did not mention you in this acknowledgment, I am truly sorry . . . it wasn't because I did not value your help and advice.

FOREWARD

You are about to enjoy an engaging conversation with my friend and colleague in the Alabama Chapter of the National Speakers Association, Patrick George. As I turned the pages of this charming book, I could literally hear Patrick talking.

This book explains the "head work" and mental conditioning which is absolutely essential in establishing the emotional and psychological foundation for achieving incredible goals in all phases of life.

I can attest to the fact that Patrick has "been there – done that". His unquestioned success as a professional speaker is the direct result of his living the concepts and principles he shares in this excellent book; study it, enjoy it, and do it!

Peter A. Land
MS, CSP, CMC, CPCM

FROM THE AUTHOR

This book was designed for a reader like you. Yes . . . you! Someone who wants to do more and achieve more. I recently heard that the average person only reads about 17 pages in a book and after that, they never read the book again.

Good Grief! Please don't be one of those people. Use this book . . . all 84 pages . . . to help you set Incredible goals that will have you way ahead of your classmates and your competition.

Write in this book! It's yours to use and refer back to as much as you need to. Enjoy the journey and, of course, reap all of the benefits of setting and achieving Incredible Goals.

Take care,

Patrick George

Congratulations!

Well, congratulations! Congratulations? I say this because by in large most people who buy books like this don't ever take the time to actually read them. Inside this book you will find information and insights I hope will motivate and guide you to the fulfillment of whatever you envision as "success." You are well on your way to attaining this success as you learn more about the ease of goal setting.

Volumes of materials have been written about goal setting. Most experts tend to focus on goal setting strategies. I have read many of these books and they tend to say the same things. The approach I would like to share with you is simple. I believe having a guideline to help you along the way will make the goal setting process easier to grasp.

My personal goal is for this book to inspire you, for something I have written to give you the encouragement to go the extra mile. Perhaps what follows this page will have you reaching for new goals and opportunities. My hope is that not only will you be inspired, but that you set some goals that at the moment look daring, that make you stretch, or that you plan a goal or a set of goals that will make you work harder than you have ever worked. There will be times you may not be able to see a lot of progress; this may be true for weeks, months or years. Don't be discouraged. The rewards for your time, sacrifice and dedication will arrive ... it just might not be right away. These are the kind of commitments that once you fulfill them will give you a feeling of pride, a sense of accomplishment, and the desire to set more incredible goals.

Ready to get started? Ready to move forward in your quest to achieve more? What is slowing you down? After you finish this book you will have a good idea of what incredible goals look like and be ready to set some of your own. I suggest you have a pen or pencil handy so you can jot down ideas and areas of focus as you read. It's okay, you can write in the book. At the end of each chapter there is a "Time to Apply" section. These pages are designed to help you with the goal-setting process. They can also be used as a quick reference once you finish the book and apply these lessons. This book will act as your first tool on your journey towards achieving incredible goals. OK, let's get moving … So what are you waiting for?

Setting a Solid Base

Ok. . . ok before I let you loose on the world setting Incredible Goals we need to make sure we have a solid base.

Your base? Your base for Incredible Goals would be a goal. Sounds simple but I need to be sure you, the reader, have the proper starting point before we go forward. You may be wondering how to set a goal. You start by deciding on a goal. This isn't a wish . . . a wish usually isn't attainable. A wish tends to be lofty and after breaking it down will lack relevance and will be difficult to put a deadline to. A goal has to be something that is attainable. A wish may sound like, "I want to be the smartest kid in the world." Well, how can you attain that? Also, how can that be measured? Where would you start? How long are you considered a kid? What would be the test? As you can see this would be a lofty wish . . . sounds cool, but could lead to a huge amount of frustration. A goal instead would say, "I want to have an A in all my classes as a final grade this school year." Now this can be measured, it is attainable, and it has a deadline. Keep reading, I believe you'll understand more as this chapter goes along.

How do you set a goal? Well here are the key elements you should remember. A goal should be specific, measureable, attainable, relevant, and have a timeline. In drawing the goal up you have to list the obstacles you may face. You should seek the advice of those that have achieved the goals you have set.

You have probably heard various sports figures, especially coaches, talk about having a certain goal or goals prior to the start of their official season. Certain results of their work and practice are highlighted and advertised. They in turn work towards those results during the rest of the season. That means that during practice they are reminded about what they are working towards. During each game all of their actions are geared towards achieving the goal set for the team.

I remember back when I was in high school, between my freshman and sophomore years, I decided I was going to join the cross country team. Cross country by far has to be one of the craziest sports I've ever participated in. I thought the guys ran about a mile, and since I liked to run, it was a perfect match. WRONG! Cross country for high school is three long miles. Living in South Florida, running any distance during the sweltering heat is no easy task. I quickly learned that running cross country was a huge challenge, running three miles nonstop was something that I now refer to as insanity. I tried to run three miles without practice. BOOM! That was the sound I made when I collapsed about half way through the first mile. Whose idea was this anyway? I realized I had to go about this differently. If I wanted to run three miles I had to break it down. Like setting any goals I had to specifically identify what I wanted to do. My goal was to be able to run three miles nonstop during a meet. I would be able to determine whether or not I reached this goal because it was clearly measureable by me, my teammates, and my coach.

Now that I have identified my goal, the big question is will I ever realistically be able to reach this goal? Being a sophomore and a rookie on the team I was in for loads of ridicule and embarrassment every time I stopped and gasped for air during practice. I looked to the older guys as superhuman. There was no way I was going to do this. Well I had to ask if it was really possible to run three miles nonstop or was there a trick to it. Maybe they really had a car pick them up once I was out of sight. That's what I was hoping . . . but no they actually ran the entire way. When I asked my teammates about the possibility of this becoming a reality for me, I got answers. In fact I got more than just answers. I got advice as to how to practice and how often I needed to practice. After an extended water break around the Gatorade bucket, I found out that my goal was truly attainable, and I was given advice on how to make it happen from those teammates that had done it time and time again. They told me about the things I would encounter during the course of this goal that would make it hard to achieve. One thing that still stands out is that I thought it was a speed thing. When I was younger, I was considered a fast runner. So I figured speed was the key here. WRONG! Fast in cross country only leaves you lightheaded, queasy, and with a few other conditions that are just too unpleasant to think about. Speed was not the key. I needed persistence and understanding that I was building endurance and this could not be done in a week let alone a day. Speed came with conditioning and endurance.

So I went home and wrote down my goal, and I also wrote down the advice and possible obstacles that were shared with me. I knew this was an important goal not just for me but for my team. It was able to achieve this it would positively effect the team and our chances to win meets. Was I done? No . . . after sharing this with my parents they said good . . . but we have a question. A question . . . you mean like have I lost my mind? Or did I run and bump my head already? No, they didn't ask anything like that. They asked this . . . When? When what? was my answer. When do you plan on accomplishing the three miles nonstop? This year? Next year? By the time you graduate? Oh, so I need a due date? They both felt it was necessary for me to put a deadline to this goal. OK. What would be realistic? Our next meet was the following week. I could barely walk after practice as it was. OK. I looked at the meet schedule, and I decided it would be accomplished by the last home meet at Tradewinds Park.

So I had all the proper elements of basic goal setting. I had a specific goal. The goal was measureable, and it was attainable if I followed the advice of my elder teammates and the plan I laid out. I was aware of the possible obstacles and potential problems. If I accomplished the goal it would put me in better shape physically and help the team in the process. So the goal was relevant. I wrote down the goal and kept it on my desk. That would ensure I always saw it and reminded myself of the goal daily. I wrote down that date of the last home meet at Tradewinds Park. By doing this it made the goal bound by a deadline and gave me something to push towards.

Well, are you curious as to whether or not I made it? I took the advice of the teammates. I started slow and ran the drills during practice and ran at home outside of practice. I added distance at each practice. As I added distance to my practices, cramps and sheer pain showed up. The inability to walk faster than a snail also became an issue a few times. I would come to meets thinking I was ready and wind up jogging or fast walking some stretches because of the pain and soreness. There were days when I thought I was going backwards, running shorter distances and taking more time to do it. Oh yes, I did decide one day that I was crazy and this three-mile thing was surely a sign of my illness. Maybe I had bumped my head? As the date of the meet came closer I started to think that maybe I could do this. Slowly my distance got longer. I actually started making better time. So by the time we had our last home meet at Tradewinds Park, I believed I was ready. I had practiced and had been able to measure my ability to continue running the entire three miles more and more each week leading up to the meet.

I stood at the starting line and I felt large butterflies in the pit of my stomach. My legs started hurting and my knees were threatening to go on strike. Nevertheless, the gun went off and I began the race. It seemed like it took three steps to make one real step towards the finish line. I think the sun was shining extra hot on just me that day. First mile done! Wow . . . Second mile was a blur. Here it was my last mile I felt the pressure begin to swell inside. Other runners passed by, but I hadn't stopped. Hey, to finish nonstop would be huge for me. This is the day it is going to happen, I thought. Last half mile, and I can see the finish line. I ran a bit faster, and I said to myself, let's pass at least one guy before I finish. I kicked it into high gear and managed to pass two guys as I raced to the finish line! I did it! I couldn't feel my legs and I'm not sure if I could speak at that moment . . . but I did it! I made my best time and I accomplished the goal.

So are you ready to start setting some goals? These are the foundation to all of the goals you will strive to set. The skill of setting goals properly can be applied to every aspect of your life. The goals can be for academic success, athletic success, career success . . . the list goes on. I challenge you to sit down before you go further and think about some things you would like to achieve this month, this year, or even in two or more years. Start here and then go boldly onto the following pages that will take your basic goal and give it some depth and robustness that will lead you to setting Incredible Goals. Come on . . . let's get started.

So remember your goal should be specific, measurable, attainable, relevant, and time specific.

Time to Apply -- Setting a Solid Base

Write down some specific goals you want to achieve.

Yes or No? Are they

               measurable?
               attainable?
               a wish?

When will you complete the goal(s)? How will you know?

In the space below, outline the best you can the steps needed to accomplish your goal.

List any obstacles you may forsee.

When will you start?

Who will you share this with for support?

"The secret to getting ahead is getting started."

Unknown

Incredible is the Way to Go

Goal – the objective toward which an endeavor is directed.

Gee whiz, what a dry way to say, "Set your mind to something, and make it happen." Goals are challenges to ourselves to go beyond where we are. That means going beyond our current positions in education, songs learned, friendships developed, memories experienced, books read, money earned, or souvenirs collected.

So what about incredible goals? By definition these two words come up … amazing and extraordinary. Incredible ... the word itself rolls off the tongue a little funny. It doesn't rhyme with too many words and it's not long enough to make a cute little acronym to remember it. But that's enough for me: goals that amaze you; a cut above.

Setting goals isn't easy, and setting incredible goals is a bit more challenging. Setting the bar higher will take more commitment, and it will also take more time. One thing you must remember is setting incredible goals isn't impossible.

I have read many books on successful people and organizations. People who reach a high level of success reach it by setting incredible goals.

So let's look at setting incredible goals. In other words go for the 3-point shot instead of the layup.

Incredible goals should be set to make significant change in the lives of those around you. Incredible goals are polarizing. You will know if your goals are incredible by the number of naysayers you have. A good measure as to how huge and difficult your goals are is how many people say, "You can't do it." Some of these people may mean well, some may actually have your best interest in mind. These people are trying to protect you from failure. Some are afraid you will succeed, and then they will have to reevaluate their own decisions and accomplishments. So stay the course, and enjoy the journey of setting and achieving incredible goals. Just be sure you are ready for the long haul. Remember to stay focused during this time. Incredible should mean pushing your limits and by doing so possibly inspire those around you.

Whenever I think of the word incredible, I think back to when I was younger and I got to watch my favorite television show on Friday nights. As a fan of comic books, I was glued to the set every Friday night when I was 10 years old. There was a large, green dude in purple shorts, who tossed people around. He had a temper. He was created by a radioactive accident. He was pretty strong and had huge muscles from his eyes to his feet. If you hadn't guessed, he was the Incredible Hulk. If any character lived up to his name, it was him. There was nothing ordinary about him, his origin, his strength or his ability to influence his environment. Each and every week, actor Lou Ferrigno brought the character to life, and the Hulk lived up to the title of the show. With a name like Incredible, the viewers had a huge expectation. It was going to take more than a few chairs being flipped for me and the rest of the viewing audience to feel it was truly incredible. It never disappointed. So don't let your goals disappoint either ... go beyond the average and the ordinary.

Incredible goals have to be more than good-looking stuff on paper. They create excitement. Don't just say I'm going to climb the mountain ... nice ... but how about, "I want to climb to the highest point possible?" Make your goals better than just some pretty surface matter statement. Get real, make them incredible, and then achieve them!

As you read this book and start drafting your goals, ask yourself, "How can I make this goal bigger? How can I make it an incredible goal? What will I have to do to complete this goal?" I suggest you go about setting goals and incredible goals using the following steps:

Step 1

Identify what you are looking to improve, change or accomplish. Do this first so you can establish a focal point.

Step 2

Increase the scope and focus of the goal to give it a boost: Incredible goals are above the ordinary.

Step 3

Go Deep! Yes, go deep ... reach deep within yourself to tap into all of your strengths. Go deep with your goal, don't just look at the surface of its impact, and look for its long-term and lasting effect.

Step 4

Have the tenacity of a Chihuahua ... Yes, regardless of your size or self value ... realize it's not always the size of the dog in the fight, it's the size of the fight in the dog.

Step 5

Realize when you are setting incredible goals that even though you may not get there 100%, simply because of the sheer robustness of your goal, that "close" may be enough.

Step 6
Surround yourself with positive influences. Always have access to positive people and resources.

Step 7
Be resourceful. Make the most of what you have and use these assets to propel you further toward your goals.

Step 8
Never give up.

Time to Apply -- Incredible is the Way to Go
Identify and Plan

My current interests are:

My talents and skills are:

My current goals are:

What can I apply from this chapter that will help me understand what type of goals I will be setting?

What can I apply from this chapter that will help me achieve my goals?

*"Undertake something that is difficult, it will do you good.
Unless you try to do something beyond that you have already
mastered, you will never grow."*

Ronald E. Osborn

Go Deep -- Look Beyond the Surface

Whenever we're in the position to make changes to something, we often focus on the outward appearance. Too often, we have a shining and striking surface but the roots are dirty, dingy and dull. The real goal setter will set goals that address improvements, not only on the outside, but those that challenge changes on the inside. It doesn't do you any good to clean the outside of your car if the inside is filthy and unfit to ride in or, worse, the mechanics of the vehicle are faulty.

Well, in my next story I have a great example of looking good on the outside but not being as good on the inside.

I was about 11 or 12 at this time, and both of my parents worked full-time. Whenever my mother knew she was going to be late, she would leave instructions for dinner, or we would just heat up leftovers from the previous night. This particular evening, there weren't any instructions or any real leftovers. I didn't panic; I decided that I would cook dinner for my parents and my sister. My sister usually cooked on these rare occasions, but I decided that since I was the oldest I was going to cook. My choice was fried chicken, green beans and rice. I had seen my mother fry chicken hundreds of times so it was going to be easy. I declared that this was going to be my finest hour!

I took a chicken down from the freezer and defrosted it in the microwave. I added some spices to the chicken and waited for the grease to get hot. My sister stayed clear of the kitchen. She only came by to mention where certain containers were and where the appropriate pots were stored. As the grease was getting nice and hot, I took care of my green beans and rice ... I'm still not a fan of cooking rice; this was the real rice not that minute stuff. My mother had no use for that stuff. Anyway, I think I called my sister to rescue the rice. I had to concentrate on the main course -- fried chicken! I carefully placed the nicely seasoned chicken pieces into the grease and they sizzled, just like they did for my mom. They sizzled for about eight minutes. They were golden brown, just like Mom's. Heck, Colonel Sanders was going to have to ask me for my recipe. It was pretty! Oh, the skin was crispy and the perfect golden brown. After the chicken was done I placed it on the stove, and then made muffins. Hey, why not? I had conquered the main course in less than 20 minutes. Even made sweet tea ... laying it on thick. I was never short of theatrics.

Well, Mom and Dad came home, and they could smell the chicken and muffins. Mom's first thought was nothing was burning or broken. Everything checked out. My sister set the table, and I proudly fixed a plate of chicken and sides for every-one. Dad said the blessing ... and took a big bite into that crispy golden brown and raw-on-the-inside piece of chicken! Yes, while the chicken bled red on his plate, just as each piece did for my mother, sister, me, I tried to pretend it was okay. Too much evidence. My mother yelled, "All this chicken is raw. It wasn't cooked long enough!"

It looked so pretty, but it was so raw it was almost cluck-ing beneath the pretty surface. I was so crushed, embarrassed to say the least. I saw the outside and I judged its worth by outward appearance. Mom saved the day by refrying the chicken and she made sure each piece had the proper time cooking. Mental note:

Chicken doesn't fry in eight minutes. Colonel Sanders could relax for now.

I learned a very valuable lesson on that day. Always look beyond the surface when facing new opportunities. Sometimes on the surface, things look really good and seem to meet the criteria, but with a little digging we soon may find that things aren't as they seem.

Time to Apply -- Go Deep

How can I go deeper with my original goal?

What new ideas have been created now that the original goal has been expanded?

How can I take the original goal to another level?

What will the expanded goal look like once it's accomplished?

"Only a mediocre person is always at his best."

Somerset Maugham

Tenacity of a Chihuahua
Show no Fear, Be Aggressive

We have all heard the phrase: "Have the tenacity of a Bulldog." This is usually said to motivate someone to stick with a task or goal and see it through to its completion. Well, if you are one who says this, I hate to burst your bubble but that phrase won't get it done. According to temperament information from psychologist Dr. Stanley Coren, "Bulldogs by nature aren't very aggressive at all. They just look intimidating."

The phrase should be adjusted to reveal the truly aggressive dog. Ladies and gentlemen, let me introduce you to … the Chihuahua. Yes, the Chihuahua. The tiny, little ankle-biting dog can be more aggressive than our big bulldog.

Elaine Waldorf Gerwitz in her book, Chihuahua: Your Happy Pet, states, "Fearless, tenacious, and terrierlike, the typical chi temperament is not fearful, quivering or cowering."

A Chihuahua despite its size will protect and fend off whomever or whatever threatens it. A Chihuahua has a lot of courage for a dog of its size. It shows little fear and isn't easily convinced that it can't beat the larger opponent. So accomplishing incredible goals will take the tenacity of a Chihuahua. You should be aggressive and make an all out effort to win and succeed. Regardless of your size or the size of your goal stick to it, and don't quit.

Not allowing your size or even your age to deter you from your goal is a lesson I learned back in high school. In my Freshman year I stopped by the counselor's office to inquire about some class information, and I was given a flyer about a speech contest. The contest was sponsored by the Jack and Jill organization. I didn't know much about the organization, and in those days you couldn't Google it and know the entire history in 1.2 seconds. So the only information I had was that it was an organization that supported youth. Specifically, Jack and Jill focused on youth in the Black community. The topic of the speech was, "What does family mean to you?"

I was encouraged to enter the competition ... everyone knew I liked to talk. I was told upperclassmen entered the speech contest and a Freshman didn't stand a chance. It was intimidating to say the least, but it would be a good experience nonetheless.

Prior to the competition, I worked at this speech a bit every day. I used references that were around my house. My mom sold Amway back in the '70s and early '80s so we had bookcases full of books and tapes with good stories and information. I had read a few already, so using them as reference was pretty easy.

The day of the competition had finally arrived. My mom picked me up from my after-school job and I had to change into my "nice clothes" for the competition. We drove to downtown Ft. Lauderdale, which was about 30 minutes away. As I entered the room where all the contestants were, my worst fears were realized. I was the only freshman there. To make matters worse, the returning champion was competing. He was a Senior, and he went first. By luck of the draw I spoke close to last. Everyone else spoke directly of the Black community, and I spoke about family and what I thought a family was. I talked about extended family and people who I call family. I did the very best I could.

I was able to shake the butterflies until I was done. Because I didn't mention the Black community in my speech, as everyone else had, I thought I had missed the mark. I sat down, and I saw my mother's face. She was smiling, and I was thinking, "Just like a good mother -- smile when your son just blew it!" Of course she would have never thought that, but I did.

I thought that maybe out of pity I could have scraped an honorable mention and an invitation to return the following year. I did have three more years to compete. Honorable mention was called, 3rd place was called, 2nd place was called. I was embarrassed now, left up there with nothing to show. Then 1st place was announced, and my name was called to receive the check and the award. Are you kidding me? I won. I outperformed all of those participants who were older, seasoned and from where I was standing much more prepared. I took away $100 and a trophy.

I had learned another lesson on goals and setting them big: Don't let the size of the goal or the apparent obstacles eliminate you from the competition. The odds on paper may appear like you are outmatched, but go for it with all you possess. You may be surprised at how well you do. The larger the goal is and the stronger the competition, the sweeter the triumph. Incredible goal setters realize that these are the goals that only a few people set, and even fewer stand their ground and go after them.

Being outmatched by what appears to be a greater opponent has kept many people from accomplishing their dreams and goals. A story that many are familiar with is a real time-tested example of someone going against the odds. The story of David and Goliath is the story that immediately comes to my mind.

The story as I remember it goes something like this: During ancient times the Israelites and the Philistines were at war. The Philistines had a really big warrior by the name of Goliath. It was said that this warrior stood between 7 and 9 feet tall, a giant by all accounts. All of the Israelite warriors were afraid of Goliath. Goliath made fun of the Israelite soldiers and mocked them. No one wanted to fight him. King Saul was also afraid of Goliath and his threats.

A young boy who tended sheep named David was sent by his father to check on the status of the war. David was also told to bring food for his older brothers when he went to investigate the progress of the war. David was the youngest of his brothers, and it is said his appearance wasn't that of any soldier or warrior. He was considered a mere boy. When David arrived at the battle front he saw Goliath, and he saw how afraid his brothers and the other soldiers were of him. David was offended by Goliath, and he volunteered to slay him.

David's brothers mocked him and reminded him of his duties of tending sheep. He was told that he was too small and was just a boy. David was determined, and his efforts were eventually heard by the king himself. The king, after some discussion, was convinced to allow David to fight the giant. David refused the king's armor and sword. He did, however, take five smooth stones and a slingshot to the battle. In case you didn't know, Goliath had four brothers. David made his way to the head of the warriors and challenged Goliath and his gods. David believed that God was on his side, and he would be slaying the giant in a battle.

Goliath became angry at the audacity of this boy to challenge him and mock his gods. Goliath started on his way towards David; as he did so, David grabbed a smooth rock and his sling shot. With his sling shot David slung one rock into Goliath's forehead, knocking him to the ground. David then took Goliath's sword from him and beheaded him. As for Goliath's four brothers, they ran away!

Talk about impossible odds: David was too small, too young, and had no experience as a warrior. David was not encouraged by his family or his peers to enter the battle. If anyone was to be declared an underdog David would win hands down. Instead, David was victorious despite the odds.

If you are facing a challenge in which the odds appear to be stacked against you just remember that sometimes you have to have courage and willpower. Don't back down, and don't give up. A firm key to setting incredible goals is to have the tenacity of a Chihuahua. Remember it's not the size of the dog in the fight but the size of the fight in the dog.

Time to Apply -- Tenacity of a Chihuahua

List your past accomplishments that appeared impossible to achieve before you refused to accept "no" for an answer.

What new opportunities will I explore with a new sense of courage?

"Courage is the supreme virtue, because it is the guarantor of every other virtue."

Bergen Evans

Sometimes Close is Enough

When I was about four years old I lived in Tifton, Georgia. I spent many days at my grandmother's house. Grandma had the coolest stuff ... well, if you call candy dishes with candy in them cool, especially chocolate. There was always something sweet nearby. I learned many lessons at my grandmother's. The lessons I remember were simple, and I still refer to them to this day.

The lesson of being "close enough" is one of the lessons that I recall learning from Grandma. That day started like all the others ... breakfast at home, and then around lunchtime Dad came home and brought us over to Grandma's house. I had my grandma, my mother and my little sister to fill the rest of my day. I had "special toys" over at Grandmother's house. These special toys were only at Grandma's. They weren't more expensive; they were just the toys that had a home at Grandma's. One of these toys was a yellow plastic shovel. The shovel was plain, but it became anything I wanted it to be. At times the shovel was a special aircraft that allowed me to travel through time. Sometimes it served as a weapon to fight off monsters that lived underneath Grandma's house. Today the yellow shovel was a Frisbee. Yes, a yellow oblong "Frisbee." Hey, I was four.

My grandmother was outside hanging clothes on the clothesline, and my mom and sister were inside taking a rest from the heat. I recall that Grandma was moving a little slower than usual on this day. She was recovering from a recent surgery on one of her legs and she was being careful not to bump it as she was still in some pain.

I was on the side of the house admiring how well my yellow shovel Frisbee was flying. I was very proud of how it spun and traveled over the yard. Oh, boy! This was really cool; no one had ever had a cool toy like this. I was sure of it. Well, I called to my grandmother, and I showed her the "Frisbee" and how good I was at heaving it long distances. She acknowledged it was nice, but she warned me to be careful and not toss the "Frisbee" too close to her since her leg was still healing. I continued to fling the "Frisbee," and I even started to fling it in the direction of my grandmother, not close but just where she could see how good I was with my invention. One of my throws was a little "too" close for Grandma, and she again warned me of throwing the shovel in her direction. She said if it hit her I was going to get "the switch."

For those of you reading this who aren't familiar with what a "switch" is, let me explain it in the quickest and simplest terms. A switch is a piece of Southern child-rearing equipment. A switch can be made from any branch of a small bush, plant or tree. The thinner the switch the more pain it is likely to bring. If it still has leaves on it, well that usually means it's fresh and the chances of it breaking apart before it's done being used are slim. If you grew up in the South the word "switch" brings about a reference that old and young recognize and respect. Now back to my story ...

Grandma was very serious about her leg not getting hit and that I needed to play elsewhere. I said, "Yes, ma'am." The very next throw I made was intended to be away from her but at the worst possible moment my shovel Frisbee had a malfunction! Yes ... a serious malfunction and it sailed right over to my grandmother, missing her leg by inches! So I did what any other young Frisbee thrower would have done with an errant throw ... I ran!

Why? Well, to my grandmother, that shovel was close enough. Too close was close enough for her to call my mother, me and the Lord. After I ran a brief and poorly run obstacle course, my mother, who was unusually fleet of foot on this day, caught me. Moments later, I too was calling on the Lord. I learned a valuable lesson about being "close enough."

Believe it or not, there are also rewards to being close enough. We are often deeply concerned with nailing down the nitty-gritty details of a project we take on and the overall work we are accomplishing. I am not saying doing half-work is the same as doing good work. I am also not saying that poor work habits are okay. I am saying that close can be motivating. Close can produce results. Close whets the appetite enough for us to press forward and finish. Close gets us in the proper stance, the proper direction. Close will get our competition curious. In my case, close was just as bad as if I had actually hit my grandmother. My punishment was the same; my level of fear was the same. Getting close allows us to tweak and refine; it allows the final product to be better. Morale is usually lifted when the group is getting close to its goal, and it is important to celebrate this positive momentum!

I have seen many baseball games when a batter hits a long fly ball and it lands foul by only a few yards. Usually this means that the batter swung too late or too early. He now knows that when he sees that pitch again he can make the proper adjustments, and it's sometimes possible on the very next pitch. If the adjustments are successful the ball will sail over an outfield fence, and fans will be racing for a souvenir while another run is added to the scoreboard. Close can be used to re-address the end goals and expectations. Close can be used to build motivation and achieve helpful momentum.

My next example of close being enough is a story I heard back when I was in elementary school. Getting close was inspiring and it moved two nations. At the time, I didn't know or understand the magnitude of what Terry Fox was doing, but his story is now one that gives me chills when I recall it.

The story begins when Terry was 18 years old. Terry was a teenager and deeply involved in sports in Port Coquitlam, British Columbia. He was a very good athlete. Terry received medals in diving and swimming, and also participated in basketball, baseball and cross country. He was smaller than most of his competitors so at times he had to work harder to excel. He met those challenges. Rolly Fox, Terry's father, said, "If Terry thought you were better than him at the start, he'd keep playing until he was better than you … It didn't matter what it was, he hated to lose."

So when Terry received the news that he had osteosarcoma (bone cancer), it was devastating. This form of cancer often starts at the knee and can move to the muscles and tendons. Terry was left with the decision to have his right leg amputated about six inches above his knee. At the time that was the only treatment.

At this point, no one in either Canada or the U.S. really knew who Terry was, but this would change. Terry Fox would soon become a household name.

While Terry was in the hospital receiving chemotherapy, he saw many others fighting cancer. He wanted to do something to encourage those who had cancer and their families and to bring awareness to others in Canada about cancer research. The run he planned was called the Marathon of Hope. His goal was to run from St. John's Bay, Newfoundland, to Victoria, British Columbia, approximately 4,500 miles. A couple of things make this goal incredible. First, no one had ever accomplished such a feat.

It was an incredible undertaking for anyone. Secondly, Terry's physical condition and prosthetic leg would surely make achieving this goal close to impossible for those who were unable to rise above physical challenges. Terry overcame a real challenge that by no means was easy to overcome. This should serve as encouragement to those that are dealing with the superficial challenges that live inside your head that steal your abilities even when no challenge exists.

I remember during the summer of 1980 -- as attention and publicity grew -- watching the newscasts of Terry's journey. Each night toward the end of the news, viewers would receive updates on Terry's progress. There were sometimes days without any updates. I was living in Albany, Georgia, and visited Atlanta for the summer where news from Canada wasn't always a priority. I was only eight at the time, but, to me, it was pretty incredible seeing a guy run with only one "good" leg. He ran farther than anyone I knew. I thought about how hard it must have been. That summer, my cousins and I ran around my aunt's back yard practicing our big marathon. It was a source of conversation and inspiration all summer. In fact, I later wondered whether Terry's quest served as a motivating creative force for Forest Gump's epic, albeit fictional, run.

Terry Fox had an additional goal for the run: to raise $1 from each Canadian citizen. He ran 26 miles a day through Canada's Atlantic Provinces, Quebec and Ontario. Terry was gaining enthusiasm and he was collecting money as he ran. On September 1, 1980, after 143 days and 3,339 miles, Terry had to stop his marathon just outside of Thunder Bay, Ontario. The bone cancer had spread to both his lungs.

Here is where it all comes together. Eight days after Terry had to stop, a Canadian television network organized a nationwide telethon that raised $10.5 million. By February 1981, $24.17 million had been raised, and Terry's goal was realized. Although he didn't complete his run as he had hoped and planned to do, he still managed to succeed in spreading cancer awareness and raise money for the cause.

Terry Fox died on June 27, 1981 just nine months after he ended his marathon, but his legacy lives on. Today, nearly 30 years after his death, Terry Fox is considered a Canadian national hero. Terry was named the Companion of the Order of Canada, which is the nation's highest civilian honor.

Terry Fox dared to set a goal so big that it inspired others. His goal to spread cancer awareness by running from coast to coast was extraordinary and even though he did not complete the run, the sheer quest of its undertaking inspired others. That summer, I felt my heart sink when they said he would not be able to finish. My eight-year-old brain couldn't understand the impact Terry made at that time. I thought that since he didn't finish the dream, his goal died there. That wasn't the case. Even after Terry died, his goal of spreading cancer awareness continues. As of this writing, $400 million has been raised worldwide for cancer research in Terry's name through the annual Terry Fox Run.

Terry Fox was close, and close brought about the excitement and the exposure he was looking for, just as if he had completed the journey. Sometimes close is not only enough. Sometimes close is more than enough.

Time to Apply -- Close Sometimes is Enough

List the goals that I have set that I have come close to accomplishing:

What will I need to do to get closer to completing the above goals?

Resources I need to gather and skills I need to improve to make the above goals a reality:

What can I apply from this chapter that will help me achieve my goals?

"He who moves not forward goes backward."

Johann Wolfgang Von Goethe

Surround Yourself with Positive Influences

When I was about three or four, my parents bought me a small record player. This device gave me hours of entertainment, especially when the weather didn't cooperate with my plans to play outside. Now, I realize most people reading this may not have ever owned a record -- let alone a record player -- but bear with me.

I had a decent collection of records; most of them were of the kid variety. I learned songs, the alphabet and even manners through those old records. I also had a collection of Peter Pan records, these were mainly stories narrated by a guy doing the voices of every character in the story. I had a favorite, and it was the story of Puff-N-Toot. It was a story very similar to The Little Engine that Could.

The story follows this little engine that faced adversity everywhere he turned. He was told that he was too small to over-come mountains or diversions. His chant whenever he was faced with a challenge was, "Gotta make it, gotta make it." No matter how many times I heard this record, I cheered for Puff-N-Toot. He never gave up and never backed down.

I am so glad my mom gave me such positive influences at such a young age. I think listening to that story had an impact on how I saw challenges. I didn't give up very easily and "no" was a starting point, not an ending point. I was a pumped up four-year-old, and I maintain that attitude today .You owe it to yourself: surround yourself with positive influences.

I must say that throughout my life I have had the good fortune to have people in my life who always encouraged me to do my best. I am blessed with parents who gave me many opportunities and constantly presented me with the challenge of going the extra mile. I must admit that there were times when the extra mile seemed way too far off. At least it seemed that way in my head. Whenever I made the choice to stop short of going further, it was always a decision that led to regret. I would ask myself, "Why didn't I listen?" And I'd say things to myself like, "I really could have done more." Then there were times when I took my parents' advice and I was able to experience the sweet taste of victory and satisfaction of a job well done.

As a child, my mother would often recite poetry to my sister and me. She even encouraged us to find poems that spoke to us or were just fun to read. We frequently sang songs that encouraged us and lifted our spirits. The genre ranged from a Sesame Street classic to gospel. I truly believe that having that kind of environment at an early age made a significant difference in my life.

At the end of this book you will find a few poems that are near and dear to me. Some of them were introduced to me during my early childhood. Others I have found during my speaking career when I was in need of some encouragement and positive words.

What are you allowing to influence you? Are you being influenced in a positive way by your music? Hopefully what you're reading right now will influence you in a positive way. Incredible goals are started and achieved by maintaining a positive atmosphere. Surround yourself with positive people. Maintain an avenue to someone or something that can boost you up when things get you down. I know sometimes you may find it challenging to keep positive surroundings. I know that negative is often the easy – and perhaps safest path – to follow. However, nothing great has ever been achieved by choosing to mitigate risk by staying on the "safest" path.

When setting your goals, are you driven to higher achievements by your peers or your circumstances? Have the words of a mentor or a friend ever inspired you to look ahead with anticipation? Too many times successes are derailed by negative influences mostly spoken by people we come into contact with: friends, teachers, coworkers, classmates, and family members. Even if someone has said something negative about your aspirations, you can use those words as fuel to motivate you toward reaching your goals. There is something to be said about the motivating forces that can be exploited from adversity.

Have you ever been stirred? Have you ever said enough is enough? Ever had an instructor say, "No one has ever gotten an 'A' in my class," or "You can't do it." My favorite is, "Who do you think you are?" Don't settle for the ordinary. Allow these words to stir you, motivate you, and to become a springboard ... rather than an energy draining pit.

Keeping yourself motivated is challenging. I know this from first-hand experience. I understand that as deadlines and expectations start to move in opposite directions and self doubt – the evil twin of confidence -- starts talking to you ... not whispering but shouting, it gets hard to concentrate and press on. This loud voice of defeat starts getting louder and more pervasive as time goes on. Ever been there?

You may find it hard to stay positive. During these times when the negative mental chatter, as well as the chatter from those around you, is dragging you down, I suggest you do some or all of these things to get back on track.

- Take a deep breath -- Relax
- Pray for guidance and strength or meditate
- Change your current environment (for example, change the room you are in, go outside ... take a walk)
- Take time to recall your past successes and accomplishments
- Find a movie, story, poem , speaker, or music that pumps you up and indulge in it
- Re-evaluate the goal, the time line and current obstacles you are facing
- Call a friend or a mentor and talk out your goals and your plan
- Sleep on it; sometimes rest allows you to refocus
- Work on a hobby, many times working with our creative fun side will start a spark of confidence ... I use LEGO
- Look at the goal as a whole, then break it down into "Lucky Charm" sized pieces ... when you break it down it's not so intimidating
- Attack your goal with new motivation and vigor

Get stirred up and set incredible goals and don't take no for an answer. Just setting an incredible goal can stir you. There is motivation in the commitment to see these goals to the end.

Time to Apply -- Surround Yourself with Positive Influences

List the positive things people say about you:

What do you think is positive about you?

List people you admire*

*If the people you admire are movie stars or athletes, what do you admire other than their stardom and fame.

List the traits that you admire about the people above:

Why do you feel the above traits are important?

Where is my own positive place? (This is the place where you can unwind ... it can be inside or outside. This place is most likely the place where you feel safest. This is the place your mind drifts to whenever to think of being alone.) Do you see it now?

What can I read that will keep me positive?

What can I listen to that will keep my attitude positive?

Who are the people that keep me positive?

Who do I encourage?

Suggested Reading

Some of you may have been stumped when asked what to read so I took the time to do some research.

Quote books -- there are hundreds available
Chicken Soup for the Soul -- there are over 200 titles to choose from
Faith-based literature of your choosing
Success Magazine
The Power of Positive Thinking - Norman Vincent Peale
Find Your Passion -- Arnie Warren
The Magic of Thinking Big -- Dr. David Schwartz
The Traveler's Gift -- Andy Andrews
Oh, the Places You'll Go -- Dr. Suess
The Last Lecture -- Randy Pausch

I may have stumped you again when I asked about what to listen to. Well once again I'll help you out I suggest going to iTunes and finding podcasts (which are free) by either Zig Ziglar or Les Brown to get started. From there you will find a list of speakers that frequently have messages that will inspire you.

"Positive anything is better than negative nothing."

Elbert Hubbard

Make the Most of What You Have and Shine

In our quest to set incredible goals we will be tempted to stop short because we will start to focus on what we don't have. There could very well be a laundry list of things that we believe puts us at a competitive disadvantage. We often get hung up on things like not having enough money or education, living in the wrong city, not having the "right" clothes, a lack of technology ... the list of perceived disadvantages is limited only by your imagination.

Focus on what you bring to the table and remain aware of the fact that that some of the things you lack may cause you to work harder than your competition. Indeed, your quest for fulfillment may take longer without some of the advantages others enjoy.

Take into account what you do have. Look again at your skills, your talents your resources and the one thing that you can't forget ... your incredible drive to see the goals to the end. Your drive and ambition is a variable that can't be discounted. It is true that we all have weaknesses. It is also true that we all have to rise above areas in our life that may present themselves as obstacles. The choice to get bitter or get better is yours and yours alone. Achieving incredible goals will mean you have to overcome those obstacles and focus on and make the most of what you have.

I have seen this first hand. Here's the story.

I saw this example of not dwelling in your weaknesses a few years ago when I was doing a series of presentations in Michigan and Wisconsin.

I had just started marketing myself to colleges and universities, and I had recently met a large number of college speakers and workshop presenters at a conference. One of the presenters, let's call him Daryl here, Daryl spoke about financial issues, saving for college, your first home, a better car, retirement, etc. He had a lot of information, and he was very determined. Now, at first glance you may say, "OK? What is so unique about that?" I am glad you asked! This new young speaker had cerebral palsy. He spoke very deliberately and didn't have full use of all of his fingers. He was not the stereotypical example of a presenter.

He knew his information, and he was being booked at schools and businesses around the Chicago area, where he lived. I went by his home on my way from Michigan to Wisconsin, and we had dinner. At dinner he showed me the three books he had written and the two others he was working on. I was both impressed and a bit embarrassed. Why? Well, at the time I didn't have one book written and hadn't even started writing one at that point. I hadn't even published an article. I told him, "Wow ... I don't have a book."

He answered me in his clearest voice and said, "You need to change that!" To him it was that simple. So, if you are allowing your weaknesses to hold you back from going forward ... You need to change that! It's just that simple ... right? I mean I had use of all my limbs and I didn't have any real or perceived handicap. After that night I had to take a long look in the mirror. I had to take into account all of the excuses that I was telling myself. Every time I tried to justify my lack of productivity, I kept returning to the comment, "You need to change that."

I would love to say that after that night I sat down and drafted a couple pages to my first book and wrote a few articles for some leadership magazines. Well, that didn't happen, I am sad to say. I wrote down some ideas, and I made a few drafts but those first steps never went any further. It took another four years and my attendance at a speakers boot camp to finally get the fire I needed to change my lack of productivity. I rationalized everything and since I was supplying my own mental barrier, it stood for longer than it should have.

I can say with all honesty that I understand that the fear of failure can prevent us from doing many things. The fear usually comes from us inflating our shortcomings and deflating our accomplishments and talents. If you find yourself doing the same thing, then like my friend told me several years ago: "You need to change that!"

Time to Apply -- Make the Most of What You Do Have and Shine

What are my strengths?

What have people told you that your strengths are?

Of the above strengths which ones are the most important to me?

What advantage do the above mentioned strengths give me?

What do I think my weaknesses are?

How will I compensate for my weaknesses?

Is there a weakness that I can change to a strength within the next year? If so which one is it?

"Humility is to make a right estimate of oneself."

Charles H. Spurgeon

Never Give Up

I have spent many a day reading books that were written to inspire and to motivate, only to find them fall really short of that goal. I can say that I did learn something from all of them even if it was what not to do. I have spent numerous hours watching movies that were written to uplift and inspire the audience. I must admit the movies have been hit or miss. I would like to mention the movie Pursuit of Happyness with Will Smith, based on the true story of Christopher Gardner.

According to IMDb, Will Smith's character Christopher Gardner invested in a new type of medical equipment that cost more than the current equipment on the market. This resulted in him having very few sales. Continued poor results caused a rift in his marriage and a strain on his finances. His wife eventually left him and he lost all of his possessions. He and his son were left homeless.

Chris Gardner had to work through every obstacle and set back. Gardner kept pressing on and in the end managed to triumph. His incredible will and determination are great examples for those of us who sometimes want to give up when things look desperate.

I recall seeing someone give his all when all he had was sparse in comparison to others, but he shined because it was truly his best effort. Win or lose give it all you have ... regardless of who is watching. Here is the story.

It was a rainy day in St. Augustine, Florida, and my mother was keeping two brothers this particular afternoon. The brothers were Jerry and Andy, and their parents worked with my father. The boys were close in age and were about a year ahead of me in school. I remember these two because I enjoyed their company so much. It was also a unique experience for me at the time because Andy was deaf. At first I didn't know how we could communicate or have fun. Andy could read lips, he could sign, and he also had the ability to speak some words. Once I understood how we could communicate and that he knew a lot about having fun, I realized Andy was a great friend to have over. On sunny days we would play hide-and-go-seek for hours. Andy was quite good. Like many who are differently abled, Andy had developed a keen ability to make acute visual observations. This is a perfect example of how it is natural to overcome challenges! Too much movement even in a good hiding place would have Andy tagging you out ... he was at no disadvantage!

Well, as I said, on the day I am recalling, we couldn't play outside due to the weather. The television signal was going in and out, and the lightning threatened to damage the television. My mother shut off the TV and gathered all of us around, Jerry, Andy, my little sister, and me. She told us we were going to have a talent show. We could do group acts, but we also had to do an individual performance. We prepared for it like it was going to be on TV. In all honesty it was suited for one show on TV at the time ... not Johnny Carson but the Gong Show. They would have taken us in a heartbeat. Simon Cowell would have had a field day. We rehearsed and made notes ... we were ready!

My sister did a little dance and song ... cute ... she was three. My mother read poetry, and she also sang a song. Jerry sang and danced. I attempted to tell some jokes. Andy was the last to perform. Andy stood up and started singing! He was singing a song with a familiar rhythm with his version of the words. He sang loud and long. No one knew what he was singing, but it didn't matter. Andy wanted to sing, and he gave it his all. He didn't care that deaf kids usually don't sing. He didn't care that he wasn't able to sound all the lyrics. He didn't even take into consideration that there were other things he could have done that would have been easier for him. He sang because in his heart he had a song he wanted to share. Andy got a standing ovation ... not because he was worthy of a record contract. No, we cheered Andy because his goal was to sing and he chose not to focus on what he didn't have.

At the writing of this book I have been taking Tae Kwon Do for almost three years. Last year I earned my Blue Belt, and I was on my way to learning the form, the self-defense moves, and the eskima stick patterns. One day in class during some self defense exercises I got hurt. What I thought was a temporary injury turned out to be an injury that would eventually limit my ability to practice for months. I was able to practice some days and other days – either by doctor's orders or sheer pain and discomfort – I couldn't even do the stretching exercises needed to begin practice. I was eventually slated for surgery and my attendance for class was sparse during the three months prior to surgery.

Surgery went well and after six weeks of rehabilitation I was allowed to slowly go back to training. I worked on all of my forms along with my self-defense moves. I was preparing to test before heading to my 20-year high school reunion. I was also due to be on stage for a group of students earlier that same week. I was going to use my passing of the test as an example of setting an incredible goal and achieving it. Well, to my dismay and frustration I failed the test. I failed it on the 37th move of 38! My instructor told me I was close and that he almost gave it to me.

Well, I want to say for the record that I am glad he didn't "give" it to me. I had to work harder and harder and use every inch of concentration I had, and one month later without any flaws I completed my Blue Belt test and was awarded my Purple Belt. I could have made excuses. I could have blamed the instructor for not being compassionate. No, instead I told myself that if I wanted this badly enough, I was going to fail as many times as it took to be successful. Sometimes it takes courage to be able to stare an obstacle down after it has delivered you a setback and prepare yourself to attack it again. Giving up was not an option for me ... don't let it be an option for you either.

Never give up and always go for a large incredible goal. In order for you to stay focused on what you set for yourself, I challenge you to create a personal mission statement. This personal affirmation statement is one that I encourage you to take the time and write out. This statement will serve as a reminder of what you stand for, what the goals you have set mean to you, and help you stay on the course. The statement should start with either "I," "I will," or "I can." You should post the statement by your mirror, over your bed and anywhere else you will constantly see it. Whenever you see it, read it aloud. Adopt the sense that these things, even if they aren't true at the present, will be true in the future. If we constantly tell ourselves we have confidence then sooner or later our brain says, "Yes, I am confident!"

If you take the time to fill out the "Time to Apply" sections of the book you'll have the basis for your affirmation statement already done. Instead of asking "Am I tenacious?" Your affirmation would read, "I am a tenacious goal setter." The statement is to be written with the future in mind. For example you may have identified being shy as a weakness. Your affirmation statement would read, "I am not shy, I display boldness and confidence." By writing this you are taking ownership of the thoughts that enter your mind. Or in the "Time to Apply" where you list your goals, skills, and interests you can turn that list into a statement. If your goal is to graduate with a high GPA ... your statement would read something like this: "I get good grades, and by getting good grades I will graduate with a high GPA."

At the conclusion of this chapter I have given you a place to write your own personal affirmation. The affirmation statement is a living document. This means that it can be added to as you grow and seek to accomplish more. This version doesn't have to be perfect, but it should get your mind geared up for going beyond the surface and setting incredible goals.

I firmly believe that we are all capable of setting incredible goals. We all have obstacles, and we all have people that will try to distract us or deter us. You are a unique individual that possesses talents and skills. Don't make the mistake of squandering those things for the sake of being mediocre. Also, don't hold yourself back for the sake of the crowd. NO ... push harder so the crowd will push harder to catch up to you.

So let's get started. You can't just sit there and ponder the future and what it holds. You must take action. You must start putting your plan together. You will make it happen!

I challenge you to set incredible goals and I wish you well!!

Time to Apply -- Go Deep-Again!!
No Peeking at your earlier answers

How can I go deeper with my original goal?

What new ideas have been created now that the original goal has been expanded?

How can I take the original goal to another level?

What will the expanded goal look like once it's accomplished?

"Only a mediocre person is always at his best."

Somerset Maugham

"Without continual growth and progress, such words as improvement, achievement and success have no meaning."

Benjamin Franklin

Time to Apply-Never Give Up
Incredible Goal Setters Never Give Up

Personal Affirmation Statement

Surround Yourself with Positive -- The Poems

These poems are some of my favorites. Some are from my childhood. My mother loves good poetry. On many a rainy day we would gather in the living room with a book of poems and we would all take turns reciting poems until it was time for dinner or we fell asleep.

I hope you enjoy these poems as much as I do.

The Quitter

It ain't the failures he may meet
That keeps a man from winnin',
It's the discouragement complete
That blocks a new beginnin';
You want to quit your habits bad,
And, when the shadows flittin'
Make life seem worthless an' sad,
You want to quit your quittin'!

You want to quit a-layin' down
An' sayin' hope is over,
Because the fields are bare an' brown
Where once we lived in clover.
When jolted from the water cart
It's painful to be hittin'
The earth; but make another start.
Cheer up, an' quit your quittin'!

Although the game seems rather stiff
Don't be a doleful doubter,
There's always one more innin' if
You're not a down-and-outer.
But fortune's pretty sure to flee
From folks content with sittin'
Around an' sayin' life's N. G.
You've got to quit your quittin'

This poem speaks to me more now as a professional than it ever did when I was a child.

IF

If you can keep your head when all about you
Are losing theirs and blaming it on you;
If you can trust yourself when all men doubt you,
But make allowance for their doubting too;
If you can wait and not be tired by waiting,
Or, being lied about, don't deal in lies,
Or, being hated, don't give way to hating,
And yet don't look too good, nor talk too wise;
If you can dream - and not make dreams your master;
If you can think - and not make thoughts your aim;
If you can meet with triumph and disaster
And treat those two imposters just the same;
If you can bear to hear the truth you've spoken
Twisted by knaves to make a trap for fools,
Or watch the things you gave your life to broken,
And stoop and build 'em up with wornout tools;
If you can make one heap of all your winnings
And risk it on one turn of pitch-and-toss,
And lose, and start again at your beginnings
And never breath a word about your loss;
If you can force your heart and nerve and sinew
To serve your turn long after they are gone,
And so hold on when there is nothing in you
Except the Will which says to them: "Hold on";
If you can talk with crowds and keep your virtue,
Or walk with kings - nor lose the common touch;
If neither foes nor loving friends can hurt you;
If all men count with you, but none too much;
If you can fill the unforgiving minute
With sixty seconds' worth of distance run -
Yours is the Earth and everything that's in it,
And - which is more - you'll be a Man my son!
Rudyard Kipling

I was introduced to "Invictus" recently while I was working on this book. It was the title of a movie starring Morgan Freeman and Matt Damon.

Invictus

Out of the night that covers me,
Black as the Pit from pole to pole,
I thank whatever gods may be
For my unconquerable soul.

In the fell clutch of circumstance
I have not winced nor cried aloud.
Under the bludgeonings of chance
My head is bloody, but unbowed.

Beyond this place of wrath and tears
Looms but the Horror of the shade,
And yet the menace of the years
Finds, and shall find, me unafraid.

It matters not how strait the gate,
How charged with punishments the scroll.
I am the master of my fate:
I am the captain of my soul.
William Ernest Henley

Bibliography

Gerwitz, Waldorf Elaine, Chihuaha:Your Happy Pet, Howell Book House

Holy Bible- New International Version

Wiggins, John. (December 2006). IMDb-The Pursuit of Happyness (2006). November 1, 2010 www.imbd.com/title/tt0454921/

Unknown."The Quitter."The Best Loved Poems of the American People. Hazel Felleman. New York: Doubleday, 1936. 96

Kipling, Rudyard."IF". The Best Loved Poems of the American People. Hazel Felleman. New York: Doubleday, 1936. 65-66.

Benley , William Ernest." Invictus". The Best Loved Poems of the American People. Hazel Felleman. New York: Doubleday, 1936. 73

Foss, Sam Walter." The House By the Side of the Road" The Best Loved Poems of the American People. Hazel Felleman. New York: Doubleday, 1936. 105-106

Patrick George

 **Follow me on
Facebook
and
Twitter!**

**Conferences
Keynotes
Workshops
Camps**

205.499.0294

www.patrick-george.com

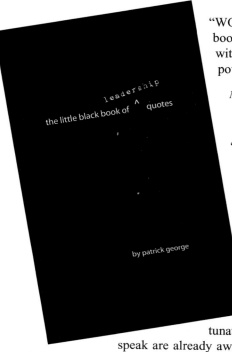

the little black book of leadership ^ quotes

by patrick george

"WOW! What a great little book. Awaken the leader within you by reading these powerful quotes."

Cara Filler
North America's leading speaker
on
Peer Pressure and Road Safety

"The Little Black Book is a true gem. The 'words to live by' are timeless and timely. No matter your age, no matter when you pick it up, a quote will jump out at you, strike a chord in you, and inspire you to act. Well done, Patrick. For those who have been fortunate enough to hear you speak are already aware of your dedication to help people move onward and upward in their life, and the Little Black Book is a true echo of your presentations. I heartily recommend Patrick's book."

Arnie Warren
Author, The Great Connection,
Find Your Passion, and Devon

"If you're ready to take your leadership to the next level, then read this inspirational book by my friend Patrick George!"

James Malinchak
Co-Author, Chicken Soup for the College Soul
Co-Author, Chicken Soup for the Athlete's Soul
Featured Expert in the blockbuster movie, PASS IT ON

Become a fan on Facebook! Search for "Little Black Book of Leadership Quotes".

"The wait is over! Leaders everywhere finally have a convenient, well organized reference book in Patrick's Quotes for the True Leader."

Gerald Jones
Motivationsl Speaker
Author of Speak Those Things

"This book is a great resource for anyone searching for inspiring and motivational quotes. Patrick has collected amazing quotes by extraordinary people and assembled them in an easy-to-read format."

Morgan Grimes
Director
Demopolis Public Library

quotes for the

T R U E
L E A D E R

by Patrick George

"Patrick was able to find quotes that will inspire both the young and the experienced."

Jonathan Sprinkles
National College Speaker of the Year
APCA

Become a fan on Facebook!
Search for
"Quotes for the True Leader".

ORDER FORM

Item	Unit Cost	Quantity	Total
Little Black Book of Leadership Quotes			
	$ 7.00 x	_____ =	_____
Quotes for the True Leader			
	$ 9.00 x	_____ =	_____
You Can't Fry Chicken in 8 Minutes			
	$ 15.00 x	_____ =	_____

Name_____

Address_____

City_____ State_____ ZIP_____

Phone_____

Email_____

Mail to
J3 Worldwide Inc.
P O Box 1307 ~ Demopolis, Alabama 36732

205.499.0294
www.patrick-george.com

Quantity discounts available on all products.

***Orders can also be placed securely
at www.patrick-george.com***

ABOUT THE AUTHOR

Patrick George is a popular motivational speaker and author of the books, "The Little Black Book of Leadership Quotes", "Quotes for the True Leader" and his newest book, "You Can't Fry Chicken in 8 Minutes but You Can Set Incredible Goals in 8 Steps". Patrick's passion for motivating people comes from his years of experience in student activities during his high school and college years. For more than 20 years, Patrick has traveled the United States and Canada motivating thousands of youth and young adults. For information on books and speaking opportunities visit http://**www.patrick-george. com/**